The Successful Book and Stationery Business

How the Kaizen Management System
can Power your Business to the Top

By John Siew

Disclaimer

The information provided within this book is for general informational and educational purposes only. The author and publisher makes no representations or warranties, express or implied, about the completeness, accuracy, reliability, suitability or availability with respect to the information, products, services, or related graphics contained in this book for any purpose. The author and publisher disclaim any liability to any party for any loss, damage or disruption caused by errors or omissions, whether such errors or omissions result from negligence, accident or any other cause. Any use of this information is at your own risk.

Table of Contents

The Successful Book and Stationery Business

Chapter 1: Reinvent Your Business

It started with a dream. You enjoyed reading and believed that starting a book and stationery business was what you always wanted to do. When a suitable opportunity presented itself, you took the plunge. Perhaps you bought the business. Perhaps you found the perfect location, observed that there was little competition and the neighbourhood needed just such a shop.

At the beginning, business was good and the financial rewards rewarding. It was a good balance of work, leisure and returns on your investment.

However, just like the seasons, the fine summer skies were gradually darkened by storm clouds as changes that took place in the business environment. More and more, books were sold online, delivered by post or courier. Many readers read books on their mobile phones. The number of new books that appeared each year increased massively due to changes in printing technology and competition has increased from rival bookstores.

In the face of such severe challenges, you are concerned about the future prospects and profitability of your business. However, as an entrepreneur, in spite of all the changes happening you continue to stay resilient and be persistent.

So you have decided to accept the challenge. You decide to study and adopt new strategies that would enable you to be compete in this new environment.

What you need is a proven system that will create for your business a lean and efficient organisation that has the ability to respond to change as it takes place.

The successful business is one that is flexible with the ability to adapt. As entrepreneurs we must study each challenge with careful analysis. We must gain knowledge and insight with an open mind. Then formulate by testing and by trial and error suitable plans that can be adapted to one's own unique environment and industry.

The Solution

In the face of relentless competition, you need to position your business so it occupies a strong position in the marketplace. That is the aim of this book.

The answer is the Kaizen System. You now have the specific system that will enable your business to thrive and prosper if implemented in the way it was designed. As a small business you have to focus on your strengths. Unlike the large organizations, which are like huge ocean liners that take time to make a turn, small businesses are like speedboats with the ability to turn, speed up, slow down, and go in whichever direction the pilot wants. They have the ability to adapt quickly to industry changes and to innovate. The essence of Kaizen is continuous improvement. How is this accomplished?

The Strategy

1. Decide on a powerful Unique Selling Proposition. Your USP is your selling point, the one unique difference that sets your business apart from the many others in your specific industry. It is a great marketing tool to position and sell your product. Perhaps you offer the lowest prices, the best variety or the best customer service or some other distinguishing feature. Let your customers and prospective customers be aware of this strength.

2. Employ the Kaizen System to manage and propel rapid and sustainable performance improvement in line with you USP. Businesses have to respond as business conditions deteriorate. The Kaizen System has a twofold advantage. It will improve the performance of your business during good times and has the power to adapt and respond effectively by maximising the efficiency of all your business operations when external factors erode sales and profit margins.

Kaizen works whether we are talking of individuals, businesses, organizations, teams or even a community.

Success Story: British Cycling
The surprising power of Kaizen lies in the field of making changes for the better. It is the philosophy of searching for a tiny margin of improvement in everything. In a business, this applies to processes, products, people, promotion and every other area conceivable.

British cycling changed one day in 2003. In more than a hundred years, no British cyclist had ever won the Tour de France, the world famous cycling race.
All that was about to change when Dave Brailsford took over as performance director. Brailsford's strategy was based on the Kaizen system of continuous improvement.
" The whole principle came from the idea that if you **broke down everything** you could think of in riding a bike, and then improve it by 1 percent, you will get a significant increase when you put them all together."
Brailsford and his coaches looked at every aspect of cycling-men, machines, materials used, method. Bike seats were redesigned to

make them more comfortable. Riders were made to wear heated clothing to improve muscular performance while riding and biofeedback sensors monitored performance at all times of the workout.

They continued to search for improvements in areas that were overlooked, such as the best massage gels to aid recovery. They found the best pillows and matresses for better sleep.

Many other small improvements followed. Just five years after Brailsford took over, the British cycling team was the best in road and track cycling event at the 2008 Olympic Games, winning 60 percent of the gold medals. Bradley Wiggins became the first British cyclist to win the Tour de France.

It has been said that if you can get 1 percent better each day for one year, you end up 37 times better by the time you are done.

Pfeffer* (1994) shows how successful companies like Southwest Airlines create culture change to provide a competitive advantage. The company was able to become the top stock performer, with a 19,907 percent return from 1972 to 1992 in an industry " characterised by massive competition and horrendous losses, widespread bankruptcy, virtually no barriers to entry, little unique or proprietary technology and many substitute products and services."

The competitive advantage that the Kaizen system creates is the direct result of building learning, skill and competence in the organisation. It comes from a very productive and motivated workforce. Everyone in the organisation has the core beliefs of wasting less time, energy and resources and increasing value for the customer.

*Pfeffer,Jeffrey (1994) Competitive Advantage through People, Cambridge, MA, Harvard Business Review Press.

The future is here. As mentioned previously, to compete in the future, we need and adaptive culture. Where does one start?

The hallmarks of unhealthy or "non adaptive" cultures include arrogance, inward focus and bureaucratic tendencies. An adaptive culture has core beliefs of caring for others, including stakeholders, customers and employees and embrace processes that allow them to initiate change. This culture responds to changes- in demand, in trends, in supply changes, in technology and in taste of customers.

Corporate Culture

Nonadaptive Characteristics	Adaptive Characteristics
Internally focussed, bureaucratic Reactive Risk Averse Information flows with difficulty Low Creativity	Customer focussed Proactive Takes intelligent risks Information flows smoothly and quickly High creativity

Today, change occurs at a fearsome pace. Not only that, they affect us directly even when in far off countries owing to the interconnected nature of our global economies. This is the major reason to be adaptive in decision making.

The Kaizen culture is the answer to adapting to such fast change. Kaizen Culture believes in these aims:

- Developing strong values
- Develops people
- Build trust through shared purpose
- Works through the long term interest of all stakeholders
- Seeks out root causes
- Accept responsibility
- Expose problems
- Focus on customers
- Increase value by subtracting the unnecessary
- Produce only what is needed in the amount needed
- Inspect to confirm the process
- Scientific problem solving by everyone based on facts
- Welcome new challenges

- Continuous improvement
- Optimize the whole, not one part at expense of the whole
- Value diversity of perspective
- Dissatisfied, challenge the status quo

In the end, for Kaizen to be sustainable, the motivation to develop people must be based on a true caring and respect for individuals and society.

This is because better thinking and better people brings better results.

The list is not exhaustive and should be amended as necessary.

So how does a business, already in operation, use the powerful Kaizen system of continuous improvement?
This is best accomplished by a two step process.
The first step is to introduce the Business Development System into the business.

The people run the system.
The system runs the business.

There are 5 principles that need to be implemented to fully empower your business to deliver the desired result.

1. It aims to provide consistent results in quality and value whether for products or services. It will create discipline, order and standardization

2. People of average ability can produce good results

3. All work is properly documented in Manuals and employees work according to the standards and quality requirements set out in these manuals.

4. The system has to be robust enough to be responsive to meet a limited degree of flexibility in meeting customer needs.
5. Ideally, the system should provide all tools necessary to allow well trained employees to run the business even without the owner.

This strategy to build a competitive advantage is just as important for business giants as it is for the small business owners.

Step 2 is to implement Kaizen into your business. At the heart of the Kaizen system is the development of courage and humility. Why? These elements are essential to develop a culture of continuous improvement.

Dr. Stephen Covey in his Seven Habits of Highly Effective People, urges us to "Seek first to understand, then to be understood." Humility insists that we develop better solutions.

We will borrow Toyota Motor Corporation's Kaizen system, mainly because a major reason for their global successes the world's number 1 car manufacturer is due to the expertise at Kaizen.

The word Kaizen in Japanese is written with two Kanji characters, meaning to change and change for the better. It has roots in ancient China going back to the Qing dynastic period.

A major issue in a business, whether it is a bookstore or an automaker is "How do you increase productivity?" The typical answers:

Increasing the number of workers, adding machines, work overtime or working harder. It is possible to make more units by increasing equipment or personnel.

However, this will lead to increase in costs! What is the answer? By improving the quality of this work, teams can in fact produce greater quantities of quality product, using existing resources. It means working smarter and not harder.

Six Steps of Kaizen[1]

If we break down the Kaizen system into its basics, we find there are six necessary steps.

- Discover improvement potential
- Analyse the current methods
- Generate original ideas
- Develop an implementation plan
- Implement the plan
- Evaluate the new method

It does not end there, because the new method always has the potential for improvement, too. So the cycle is continuous, always aiming for better outcomes and results.

*(2012) Art Smalley, Toyota Kaizen Methods in Toyota by Toyota, Toyota and Francis Group

Step 1: Discover improvement potential

Improvement potential exists because there will be a difference between what is the current situation and what is potentially possible. Take for example car design. Cars today are better and more economical than those made in 1960. We call this a gap or shortfall.

Second, observe the workplace. Much research is needed to understand a process. Accurate measurement of each part of a process is needed. Strive to be AQD, meaning analytical, quantitative and detailed in data collection.

The third area is to identify all forms of waste that exist in that area.

Finally, make sure to organise, arrange and clearly label all components in process, whatever they may be.

For a book and stationery shop an important area can be to make it very easy for customers to find all the many items parents want to buy for school at the start of a school term.

Step 2: Analyse the Current Method

There is no one best way to analyse. The main thrust is to study the process or processes in operating the business,

- Make a detailed and careful analysis of the steps in a process. Ask how best to carry out each action.
- Question. Find out what, when, why, where, who and how it is being done
- Use the ECRS method. Can any steps or things be eliminated, combined, rearranged and simplified? If we seek hard enough, we will find them.
- Time and motion. The aim is to find and establish an analysis known as standardized work. The objective? Try to create the right rate and method to synchronize supply to demand. Done right, work elements are aligned to demand so as to eliminate overbuilding or excess inventory.

In a stationery business, having accurate data on the rate of demand for each and every item will reduce overstocking or understocking of goods to the minimum and arrive at the best quantities to order for every item for every season of a year.

Step 3: Generate Original Ideas

Step 3 is to generate original ideas for improvement. The important thing is not to stifle the creative process.

Often have preconceived ideas of what will work and are quick to make conclusions. Suspend judgement. Do not be fearful of failure. Test and experiment. Generate many ideas. From these choose the best ones.

Checklists are another good tool to adopt in idea creation. Ask many questions. The 5W 1H method of questioning should be used. Be flexible in our thinking. Can we reuse, enlarge, reduce, substitute, rearrange, reverse or combine?

Brainstorming works too. Encourage the team to be free to contribute ideas. Work as a team.

Step 4: Make a Kaizen Plan

Any improvement ideas that management has decided to implement should be carried out immediately. However, for successful outcome, it is necessary to develop a plan to guide the steps of the implementation. These steps are required.

- What is the action to be done? Provide specific and clear instructions
- Who will implement the action. It will be necessary to appoint a leader to take charge, be accountable and to coordinate steps
- A dateline for completion
- The expected result from the change
- Where the actions are to be carried out
- Measure the results and analyse if the change has resulted in measurable benefits. Assess the success or failure of the change.

Step 5: Implement the Plan

The plan creation process has been completed. What will be the time sequence and stages of implementation? You may need to develop short, medium and long term steps or actions. As a bookstore, you may have decided to set up a coffee place for browsers to relax and examine books before purchase. The short term plan may be to set up a basic coffee stall with very limited space. In the longer term if the idea works out successfully you may expand it to include a full offering of food items for people who want to have a quick meal as they browse the store.

- They may be a need to explain and coordinate with those charged with the implementation. Is there a process to update and review as the need arises?
  Often, problems arise and have to be anticipated and solutions have to be found. There is a need to train staff on how to act in a situation where changes happen. Kaizen means change. There needs to be a training plan and maybe a training manual.
- Do not give up when unexpected problems arise. Rise above them and believe they can be overcome. As necessary, amend and make changes as appropriate. Keep good records and data and test again and again.

Step 6: Verify the Results

Whether we have implemented a good change will depend on the outcome. We will need a standard or benchmark against which to measure results.

If the change has been positive, we need to find out by how much. Was there an increase in output? A reduction in costs? A saving of time and labour?

These questions have to be answered honestly, then we can assess if our goals are met.

If not, further changes may be needed. What is our next step to find alternate methods or adjust our processes. If results are met, can we use the change made in other parts of our business operation. How do we sustain the gains?

Critical Systems in your Book and Stationery Business for Kaizen Systems

Information Systems

Information on customers' preferences, cost information, data on the margins earned from the different kinds of products, the results from promotion and marketing strategies and tactics have to be collected. They need to be systematically analysed and improved on a constant basis to discover the unmet needs of different groups of customers.

Good information systems will revolutionise your business practices. Businesses too need to collect information on competitors so as to develop marketing strategies to compete because change is a fact in the marketplace.

Lead Generation System

Every business needs a constant stream of customers. Most businesses do not make efforts to build a growing customer base. The most popular method of getting people through the door is through newspaper ads. Adding your company on the local area webpages works well for many businesses who serve a certain geographical area.

Every business has to generate leads to grow the customer base. What is a lead? A lead is any person who has shown an interest in the company's products or its services.

All businesses need new customers because some existing customers will leave for one reason or another. To increase profits, you will need to build the customer base.

Take a typical pie shop. Existing customers on average will buy say, X number of pies each day. If the pie shop wants to increase profits, she needs to increase sales, and that means securing new customers and converting them into long term customers through the process below:

Strangers→ Visitors→ Leads→ Customers and Promoters

It means you have to:

Attract to Convert, then Close and Delight

There are many tools these days to build a list of loyal customers

1. Build a website- A good website is a great way to get the word out. Show as much information as possible of your products and services. Include a Call to Action (CTA) wherever suitable, inline, bottom of post or even on side panels.

2. Manually collect information- Do this for walk in customers, phone in customers, and from the internet. Treat them with great value. Contact them and make offers to encourage them to return with good offers.

3. Social Media- Connect with your community using social media. Use Facebook bio links and bitly URLs on Twitter.

4. Blogs- Blogs which are written by authoritative sources are great to build trust and confidence in your product or service. You can tailor the blog to your end goal to promote an offer or capture contact information.

5. Product Trials- Offer them to try out your product or service for free for a limited period. If they like it they will continue with a paid service.

6.   Referrals- Provide your customers with excellent products and services and your referrals with roll in.

7.   Deal making sites- There are many good ones these days- Grab A Deal, Groupon, One A Day and many more.

8.   Email List- Build your email list. Sent them special offers. Showcase your products and services.

Lead Generation Using a Lead Magnet

You can set your own system to generate leads using a lead magnet on your website. Value the visitors to your website. Many may become loyal customers.

1.   Reach visitors searching for a product or service with your website, blog or other channel

2.   The visitor if he is interested in your free gift or offer will click on the image/button/message that encourages them to click

3.   If you have linked the offer to a landing page which has been set up with a form that enables you to capture their details you will be able to get this important information. You can ask for name, email, phone and other personal information as

you think your prospects will be comfortable to provide.

4.   Your free gift or lead magnet is something of value or interest to the customer. It can take the form of an ebook, course, template or other gift.

Channels to build Leads

From these channels, send prospects to a Landing page to download the free gift. At the same time you are collecting leads.

A business that does not have a quality control system will produce results that are not consistent. If a bakery sells bread that is left over from yesterday at normal price, the customer will feel cheated. The business that has robust quality control will gain a great advantage over is competitors.

1 Goals- Start with the end in mind. All businesses focus on customer satisfaction. You need a strategy that delivers value to the customer and to make this process one of constant improvement.

2. Train the staff to emphasize quality first- A quality management system must ensure that staff be well versed with their functions on the job. McDonalds ensures bread is fresh every day. Quality of product must deliver value every time.

3. Examine Existing Processes- Workflow in the business has to be able to give high quality results. Current methods have to be examined and any improvements to processes updated regularly. Changes in demand, technology and taste need to be observed and changes made as required.

For example, restaurants have to adjust their menu to consider changes in demand for healthy meals and speed of preparation.

Grocery stores have to be able to maintain freshness of their produce to avoid losing their customer base.

4. Standardize-The easiest way to ensure quality is to standardise everything from start to finish. There needs to be a manual so that procedures and processes can be carried out according to the manual instructions. E.g. If a new employee joins a bakery, she has to follow the exact process to ensure the bread is consistent in terms of weight, shape, moisture, and combination of ingredients to always produce an excellent loaf.

5. Checkpoints- You need to institute checks at unexpected times so processes are followed and adhered to, that the materials used are up to standard, that there are no lapses in quality of product.

6. Flexibility- You need to be flexible as well. In a world of constant and often unexpected changes, you have to be alert to these changes in local, regional and international trends and be flexible enough to meet the challenges that will arise.

A way to keep in touch with your customer preferences and changes in taste is customer feedback using social media and customer surveys. Ask for frequent feedback on their needs and suggestions or improvement. Then evaluate them and be nimble to make change part of quality improvement programmes.

In the internet age we live in, social media is an absolute must for all small businesses. The old marketing was mostly one way- businesses had to reach out to show their offers in the newspapers, magazines, TV.

Today customers desire to engage with the businesses they patronise. Think two way communications, forming relationships that create win-win customers.

1.   Choose your Platform- think of the customer first. Where do they go online to search for information? What sites do they use? Do research to find out their favourite social media sites. If they favour Facebook, Twitter, and similar, use them to connect with current and future customers.

2.   Encourage Engagement- You need to set up a system to provide valuable information about your product or service. This is especially important for products that undergo changes often, or new models are available. Ask questions, do research on your customer preferences. Doing so will help

position your business in prospects/customers minds.

Example, if you sell a skin care product you can provide informative posts on diet, exercise and tailor specific skin care products to people with different issues with skin care

3.   Produce a Calendar for Marketing- People will buy more products and services on special days and occasions. Special days like Mother's Day, New Year, Christmas and the like are great opportunities. Offer special discounts and work with suppliers to buy in bulk the most popular products bought during these seasonal periods. Offer gifts to customers on their birthdays to build long term goodwill that pay dividends in the long run.

A calendar will help make your marketing systematic and organised. Campaigns can be planned and tailored to it specific events and be season appropriate.

4.   Build a Following and a Community- To ensure the long term success of your business, focus on building a community of raving fans.

A restaurant business can build a base of loyal customers by making them feel special whenever they patronise your business. Always seek to make each experience highly satisfying for the customer.

On social media, satisfied customers gladly share their good (and bad) experiences. These days phone users use What's App to take photos of the food in a restaurant and rate it 5 stars if they are happy and satisfied.

Restaurant can also reach out to influential social media users. Offer them free meals and ask for reviews.

Most Popular Social Media Sites

1.   Facebook- It is estimated more than 65 million businesses use Facebook.

Almost all content format works great on Facebook, whether text, images, videos and stories. It is great for starting interactions and building relationships with your customers. It is also good for advertising your products and services to prospects and customers.

2.   You Tube- The most popular video sharing platform. Many people watch the videos daily and you can create a You tube Channel for your brand, upload videos for your subscribers to view, like,

and share. It is a medium that appeals to the senses, visual, auditory and creates powerful emotions in the minds of consumers if the message is done well. Use it to educate customers and promote your products.

3.   What's App- This is used by people in more than 180 countries. An extremely popular method for families, friends, groups to keep in touch and very easy to use.

It is now used by businesses of all kinds to communicate with customers. People love to share pictures of food and food sellers simply love the reach of this app. You can set up a business profile, provide customer support and advertise to your customers.

4.   Messenger- This used to be a messaging feature with Facebook. It is now a standalone app. It allows you to advertise, create chatbots which are great for convincing prospects, clear doubts and answers their questions quickly.

5.   WeChat- The most popular app in China. A powerful system that allows users to shop online and make payments, transfer payments money, make reservations and book tours.

6.   Instagram- This is a social media app for sharing live videos, video photos and stories. Build an Instagram business profile and schedule posts using third party tools.

7.   QQ- Popular with Chinese, it is also used in many other countries.

8.   Tumblr- This is a microblogging and social networking site for sharing text, photos, videos, audios and more. You can make 7 kinds of Posts on Tumblr.

9.   Twitter- This is a quick messaging system. Apparently it is often used as a customer channel. You can reach many at the same time if you build a following. Keep in touch with customers

You can use it to offer special deals to good customers and also to promote products and build quick cash flow. Customer service tools such as Buffer Reply are available to help manage social customer conversations.

Other channels to reach customers are Reddit, Ozone, Tik Tok, Linkedin, Snapchat, Pinterest, Line, Telegram and Medium. Analyse these social media sites and determine the best ones to use to connect with your customer base.

With the large number of social platforms being used today, small businesses may have a hard time connecting with new customers. A number of third party apps are available to make social media marketing lucrative and useful for promotion. Some of these are:

Buffer- This tool enables businesses swamped by multiple social media accounts they must manage. They minimise the time spent on social media, allows queueing of posts, organize them and make marketing manageable.

Other tools- Sendible, Maxservice, Storyheap, Unsplash and a host of other providers.

Every small business has to have systems to generate cash flow in a short time as the need arises.

Every business has to meet financial commitments as they arise, such as salaries, rent and so on. There is a need to speed up the conversion of sales into cash quickly and increase the spread between the inflow and the outflow of cash.

1.   Follow up and follow up again- If a prospect has expressed interest, you have to follow up as soon as possible. If the prospect asks for more information, provide as much as you can quickly. Answer all their queries to their satisfaction. People are more likely to buy once their objections are addressed and understanding increases. Provide evidence of the performance, giving the full benefits, specifications, features in clear, simple language. Show before and after pictures of the work you do. If they do not respond make sure to follow up.

2.   Closed Door sales- Write to your customer or email them with an invitation to an exclusive sale

where only past customers are invited. This sale can be after normal hours and the bargains are especially good.

2.1 Give it an air of exclusivity, make people feel special

2.2 Genuine discounts and offers so they do not see it as just another cheap sale which is being held 10 times a year.

2.3 Give them the opportunity to bring a friend along

3.   Provide a Rain Check Service-Many small businesses often run out of stock on a particular model, or clothing size or colour. A rain check service will make for happy customers who will feel that this business genuinely tries to serve and not merely looking after its own interests.

It builds long term relationships and lifetime customers and you will be rewarded with more support from them.

4.   Discounts- Sales are becoming very common these days. You can offer 30% or 50% off but it does not mean much. If you want to differentiate

your sale from other competitors, you need to have a rational justification for the price reduction.

Example, your book and stationery business should offer:

Discounts perhaps twice a year so your customers will know it is not just another gimmick, but a genuine and worthwhile sale.

Only loyal and more frequent customers get better discounts. Meaning you have to keep records of customers and select those who give you the most business.

5. An Advance Sale- Loyal and best customers get the priviledge of being offered an advance sale where they get first choice. They could be notified one day ahead of the sale for the general public.

6. Allow Payment Terms or Financing- For higher priced items, this method will definitely boost sales and cash flow. Allow customers, especially those who are hesitant to make a deal, to pay for the product or service over a period of time.

7. Point of Sale Material- This is often a great method to add to your cash flow as it is a proven way to help indecisive shoppers make a decision. With so many competing products the consumer ill frequently decide to buy a product that "stands

out". It is also a good promotion tool as you can have a special to sell more of those brands that give you a better margin.

Bin labels are often available from suppliers or you can produce your own. Make them clear and colourful and list other products that are commonly purchased with that item to increase even more sales.

e.g. if you sell ACE brand paint brushes, suggest suitable papers for drawing, accessories used by artists, and other suitable products and ingredients that are related using P.O.S.

8.   Treat Customers like Gold- Few businesses try to build rapport and treat their customers as someone special. More often than not, when you walk into a restaurant, there is no greeting. The waiter sometimes makes them wait for the menu. No efforts are made to determine the customers' food preferences.

Train staff to be friendly, serve the customer well and try to be as helpful as you can.

Make them feel they are assured of a good experience every time so they will return often

9.   Encourage People to Buy More- Offers such as Buy one, get one free, 4 for the price of 3.

You do need to ensure margins are profitable. If you are able to sell large quantities, you can negotiate better prices from suppliers.

It increases turnover, gets rid of old or older stock, ensures items close to expiry are sold off and will increase cash flow to stock new items.

They are good crowd pullers. Once in the store, people will often buy more.

10. It is important to find out facts: Study all aspects of the business. It is important to understand every revenue and cost area so that decisions are based on proper analysis and not guess work.

Everything from the results of advertisement, sales of all products, margins for the product or service, cost of production, demand, supply, customer satisfaction have to be analysed on a regular basis and changes made if necessary to improve margins and processes.

1. Look at each area of the business individually

2. Test and measure the response and result to every ad.

3. Practise consistent improvement in every area of the business but do not compromise quality.

To increase your profits in the year ahead, you need to focus attention on the critical areas that drive profit growth. Then act to deploy systems thinking into a profit growth system.

These critical areas are:

1.   Customer Retention Rate: Overtime, some customers will not return, some leave the area, while others may no longer require the product. It is like money falling from a hole in the pockets.

Smart companies understand that all customers have lifetime customer value. They are much more valuable than the amount they spend on their first visit.

They are a valuable asset. Think bread and butter. How much will you spend on these in your lifetime? Not only that, satisfied customers will refer your business to their friends and contacts.

2.   Lead Generation: Every business needs to bring in new customers in order to grow. In the past, businesses used print and billboards to reach

prospective customers. Today, social media and the internet play a dominant role.

3. Conversion Rate: This is the proportion of leads that converts into new customers as a result of your marketing efforts. Businesses aim for high rates of conversion.

4. Average Spend: Also known as Average Revenue.

Total Revenue (or Total Sales)/

　　　Number of Customers

= Average Spend

5. Gross Profit: This is Revenue from Sales minus the Cost of Goods sold but before overheads.

Revenue-Cost of Goods Sold=Gross Profit

We shall examine the case of a small business to determine how they may use systems to optimize operations and double their profit in a year.

The Cove is a small retail book and stationery store in a suburban area. They have an annual revenue of $1,500,000 and earned a gross profit margin of 40 % of sales. This translated to a figure of

$600,000. They have fixed costs of $160,000 and variable costs of $240,000.

Net profit for last year was $200,000.

The Systems Strategy to Double Profits

To increase profits, The Cove adopts a system that leads to them to implement the following actions:

Retention Rate

- Created a system to reward loyal customers
- Used their Information systems to survey and understand customer needs
- Started a system to train staff to educate customers on the quality of their products and the best way to present these products

The result- An increase in retention rate from 70 to 80 customers in the last year.

Lead Generation

- Using a lead magnet in the form of a FREE Ebook

1000 Jokes, Puzzles and Optical Illusions

Result- Increased leads obtained from 10 to 12%

Average Spend

•   Created a new line of personalised jewellery for young professionals from work and social functions that emphasized uniqueness and contemporary tastes.

Result- Increased average spend by 10%

Gross Profit

•   Analysed their information systems to determine items that provided the best profit margins.

•   Increase productivity by offering staff an incentive system to boost sales

THE COVE PROFIT GROWTH PLAN

	Current $	Increase	After * $
Last year	1000		1,000
Retention%	70	10%	80
This Year	700		800
Leads	500	10%	550
Conversion%	10%		12%
New customers	50		66
Total this year	750		866
Average Spend	2000	10%	2200
Sales	1,500,000		1,905,000
Gross profit %	40		43%
Gross Profit	600,000		819,236
Expenses	400,000		420,000
----------------------------			------------
Net profit	200,000		399,276
================			=======

\# Refers to the profit potential that can be realised if The Cove was able to successfully implement the systems they have decided to use to improve business operations.

They will get the results they want if they are prepared to respond to the changing marketplace. They need to be flexible and stay focussed.

They also need to adopt the Pareto Principle in analysing the business and implementing strategy. The Principle states that 80 % of the results come from 20% of the actions. That applies to all their systems from lead generation to improving gross profit margins.

Building a Kaizen culture in your business is the first step. It is not enough. When the leaders of an organisation change, will it survive?

Being adaptable is the key to long term success. Often a business falls back to old habits. Jon Miller et al (2014)[*2] says only about 5 percent of companies will continue to sustain the Kaizen culture. They believe that to sustain change, it is necessary to supply sustenance to develop people's thinking behaviour with the intention to make continuous improvement a habit. The key? Practice makes perfect. By building habits and routines, by continuous repetition of the maintenance and improvement cycles this will reinforce the change in behaviour.

Use the Cue-Routine-Reward system to produce a habit loop that is both systematic and provides tangible results. If a piece of work is found to be substandard (Cue), then go to the stage of gathering the team to solve the problem.

(2014) Miller,Jon; Wroblewski, Mike and Villafurte, Jaime, Creating a Kaizen Culture,McGraw Hill

Here we use Kaizen methods to resolve the issue (Routine). The result is problem solved, and target achieved. (Reward). This positive result further reinforces Kaizen thinking and action.

Workers need to practice these habits on a daily basis and management needs to support and encourage the practice. When a worker sees an issue, a defect or a fault that fails a standard of performance, he must stop, request assistance to get the issue resolved.

The end goal is to seek solutions that result in a win for all parties. Being transparent is vital, focus on fixing problems, on developing better more robust systems.

The business has to deliberately set time and effort for Kaizen activities. We cannot be so busy sawing that we have neglected to sharpen the saw.

Kaizen has the power to change your business in a powerful way through continuous improvement. There is a principle that says 80 percent of our results come from 20 percent of our efforts.

In business, I believe marketing and customer relationship management is the 20 percent we need to concentrate and focus on.

An example would bring out the value in providing great service in business.

When I bought my first car, a Toyota Corolla, I wanted the best to maintain it. Most garages and auto repairers can do a "reasonable" job and that includes Toyota Service. I wanted a better service, one that will go the extra mile. So I searched and finally found one that did.

Jack (not his real name) was nothing short of outstanding in his trade. I liked his easy manner, likableness, respectful attitude and knowledge of the car mechanics from the start. He was the owner of a small repair shop. Trained as a Toyota serviceman, his work ethics were excellent and his understanding of how cars work unparalleled. That included many makes of cars.

Each time I called to book a service, or personally brought the car in for service/repairs, he was always prompt to come. No waiting around to be serviced as in some auto shops. He would quickly diagnose the problem and do it accurately. Then he would give a quote, usually very close to actual costs based on initial inspection. He would take time and trouble to explain the problem in simple terms and help me appreciate how the problem arose and provide tips and ideas on how to drive, brake, maintain and care for the car, engine and other systems so as to maintain and increase the lifespan of the car. This would give good resale value, an indication of mindfulness.

Whenever a job was complete, he would show me the parts replaced so I could be sure genuine parts had been used. The invoices he showed were very detailed, in order of priority all parts used in repairs even down to the smallest parts. Once the job was done, the car never needed to be sent back for adjustments, or retuning and mistakes were never made.

Without learning about Kaizen or marketing, he put in practice the basic concepts and principles in all work that he did. As a small business owner you do not have the huge resources of major corporations. However you do have one strong advantage-the flexibility to make changes and respond quickly to change.

Imagine a ship, a supertanker, more than a 100,000 tons on the high seas making a turn. It's size and weight means it will take a lot of fuel and much time to steer it in a different direction. Your small business, like a speedboat makes a change in direction relatively quickly and easily.

Secondly, large organisations are encumbered by bureaucratic layers of management and seldom listen to managers on the ground, those in direct contact with the customer. Such was the case of Ebay.

Ebay was the leader in online auctions. Yet they lost out to Taobao in the Chinese market because they did not take the time and the trouble to understand what the Chinese users wanted, which was "freemium", where basic functions were free while charging for premium services.

Bottom line for your business development is that:

The Kaizen system of continuous improvement should be implemented for ALL the functions of your business. However, most attention should be focussed on marketing and customer relationship management.

If you adopt Kaizen to make continuous improvement to all these areas you will be the best in your niche

- Are all customers, prospects always greeted with respect, courtesy and prompt service provided?
- Is your business easily found on the internet, with information on business hours, location, contact information?
- Is your website informative and easy to negotiate, with all important information on products and prices, new items, services offered
- Is there an online catalogue?
- Does the business collect information on all customers, existing and new. Do all staff do their best to understand the needs and wants of customers? For a book and stationery store, you have to be able to "tailor" information to meet the specific needs and wants of the individual customer. This is especially true for

books so that you know their interests in the area of the kinds of books they read, genre age group and so on. Ask customers in person, by surveys and other methods.

- Email your customers and provide them with deals, information on items of interest, new books, answer their questions
- Treat like gold the 20 percent of customers who provide 80 percent of you sales. They should be give special privileges in the form of loyalty discounts or a special discount when their purchases reach a certain predetermined amount.
- If CDs, VCDs, records are being sold, is there an area for them to try out and test these materials?
- Keep in touch with customers using social media. Provide information on store products, write articles in blogs. Invest in a good system to assist customers quickly find everything you sell in your store
- Do you offer refreshments or is there a coffee area, preferably free for customers to relax, browse and go through the books.
- Provide adequate parking, free if possible
- If books of stationeries are not in stock, offer to make orders for the customer and contact

them to collect as soon as possible(depends on value of item)

- Keep in touch with the technological side of your business. This is where businesses of the future will compete effectively or become obsolete. You need to find your special niche to compete. Use technology to continuously improve efficiency and meet a customer base that wants to shop using computers and mobile devices.

- Provide good quality products at competitive prices. There are consumers, of course who want cheaper items, for example, filing systems, so it is best to offer a range of each item. Cater for economy the economy minded and those who want better quality.

Right now, you have the roadmap to creating systems that if crafted and implemented correctly, will put your business head and shoulders above the crowd.

All of us know that no matter how well our business is doing, there are ways to make improvements. The reason why business people do not change is fear of change and being too busy working on daily tasks to spend some time to learn new and better ways to make their business more profitable and in turn life more satisfying.

Now you have the tools and motivation to make the change and see your business soar.

www.ingramcontent.com/pod-product-compliance
Lightning Source LLC
Chambersburg PA
CBHW030524220526

45463CB00007B/2714